WILLIAM SHAKESPEARE'S
POEMS AND QUOTES

2013 by Ink Walk Book Publishing

ISBN-13: 978-0615881157 (Ink Walk Book Publishing)

ISBN-10: 0615881157

Ink Walk Book Publishing
Woodland Hills, CA. 91367
www.inkwalk.com

Table of Contents

3

A Fairy Song

Over hill, over dale,
Thorough bush, thorough brier,
Over park, over pale,
Thorough flood, thorough fire!
I do wander everywhere,
Swifter than the moon's sphere;
And I serve the Fairy Queen,
To dew her orbs upon the green;
The cowslips tall her pensioners
be;
In their gold coats spots you see;
Those be rubies, fairy favours;
In those freckles live their savours;
I must go seek some dewdrops
here,
And hang a pearl in every cowslip's
ear.

William Shakespeare

A Madrigal

Crabbed Age and Youth
Cannot live together:
Youth is full of pleasance,
Age is full of care;
Youth like summer morn,
Age like winter weather;
Youth like summer brave,
Age like winter bare:
Youth is full of sports,
Age's breath is short,
Youth is nimble, Age is lame:
Youth is hot and bold,
Age is weak and cold,
Youth is wild, and Age is tame:-
Age, I do abhor thee;
Youth, I do adore thee;
O! my Love, my Love is young!
Age, I do defy thee-
O sweet shepherd, hie thee,
For methinks thou stay'st too long.

William Shakespeare

Aubade

HARK! hark! the lark at heaven's
gate sings,
And Phoebus 'gins arise,
His steeds to water at those
springs
On chaliced flowers that lies;
And winking Mary-buds begin
To ope their golden eyes:
With everything that pretty bin,
My lady sweet, arise!
Arise, arise!

William Shakespeare

Bridal Song

ROSES, their sharp spines being
gone,
Not royal in their smells alone,
But in their hue;
Maiden pinks, of odour faint,
Daisies smell-less, yet most quaint,
And sweet thyme true;

Primrose, firstborn child of Ver;
Merry springtime's harbinger,
With her bells dim;
Oxlips in their cradles growing,
Marigolds on death-beds blowing,
Larks'-heels trim;

All dear Nature's children sweet
Lie 'fore bride and bridegroom's
feet,
Blessing their sense!
Not an angel of the air,
Bird melodious or bird fair,
Be absent hence!

The crow, the slanderous cuckoo,
nor
The boding raven, nor chough
hoar,
Nor chattering pye,
May on our bride-house perch or
sing,
Or with them any discord bring,
But from it fly!

William Shakespeare

Dirge

COME away, come away, death,
And in sad cypres let me be laid;
Fly away, fly away, breath;
I am slain by a fair cruel maid.
My shroud of white, stuck all with
yew,
O prepare it!
My part of death, no one so true
Did share it.

Not a flower, not a flower sweet,
On my black coffin let there be
strown;
Not a friend, not a friend greet
My poor corse, where my bones
shall be thrown:
A thousand thousand sighs to
save,
Lay me, O, where
Sad true lover never find my grave
To weep there!

William Shakespeare

Fairy Land ii

YOU spotted snakes with double
tongue,
Thorny hedgehogs, be not seen;
Newts and blind-worms, do no
wrong;
Come not near our fairy queen.

Philomel, with melody,
Sing in our sweet lullaby;
Lulla, lulla, lullaby; lulla, lulla,
lullaby!
Never harm,
Nor spell nor charm,
Come our lovely lady nigh;
So, good night, with lullaby.

Weaving spiders, come not here;
Hence, you long-legg'd spinners,
hence!
Beetles black, approach not near;
Worm nor snail, do no offence.

Philomel, with melody,

Sing in our sweet lullaby;
Lulla, lulla, lullaby; lulla, lulla,
lullaby!
Never harm,
Nor spell nor charm,
Come our lovely lady nigh;
So, good night, with lullaby.

William Shakespeare

Fairy Land iii

COME unto these yellow sands,
And then take hands:
Court'sied when you have, and
kiss'd,--
The wild waves whist,--
Foot it featly here and there;
And, sweet sprites, the burthen
bear.
Hark, hark!
Bow, wow,
The watch-dogs bark:
Bow, wow.
Hark, hark! I hear
The strain of strutting chanticleer
Cry, Cock-a-diddle-dow!

William Shakespeare

Fairy Land v

FULL fathom five thy father lies;
Of his bones are coral made;
Those are pearls that were his
eyes:
Nothing of him that doth fade,
But doth suffer a sea-change
Into something rich and strange.
Sea-nymphs hourly ring his knell:
Ding-dong.
Hark! now I hear them--
Ding-dong, bell!

William Shakespeare

A Lover's Complaint

FROM off a hill whose concave
womb reworded
A plaintful story from a sistering
vale,
My spirits to attend this double
voice accorded,
And down I laid to list the sad-
tuned tale;
Ere long espied a fickle maid full
pale,
Tearing of papers, breaking rings
a-twain,
Storming her world with sorrow's
wind and rain.

Upon her head a platted hive of
straw,
Which fortified her visage from the
sun,
Whereon the thought might think
sometime it saw
The carcass of beauty spent and
done:

Time had not scythed all that youth
begun,
Nor youth all quit; but, spite of
heaven's fell rage,
Some beauty peep'd through lattice
of sear'd age.

Oft did she heave her napkin to her
eyne,
Which on it had conceited
characters,
Laundering the silken figures in the
brine
That season'd woe had pelleted in
tears,
And often reading what contents it
bears;
As often shrieking undistinguish'd
woe,
In clamours of all size, both high
and low.

Sometimes her levell'd eyes their
carriage ride,
As they did battery to the spheres

intend;
Sometime diverted their poor balls
are tied
To the orbed earth; sometimes
they do extend
Their view right on; anon their
gazes lend
To every place at once, and,
nowhere fix'd,
The mind and sight distractedly
commix'd.

Her hair, nor loose nor tied in
formal plat,
Proclaim'd in her a careless hand
of pride
For some, untuck'd, descended her
sheaved hat,
Hanging her pale and pined cheek
beside;
Some in her threaden fillet still did
bide,
And true to bondage would not
break from thence,
Though slackly braided in loose

negligence.

A thousand favours from a maund
she drew
Of amber, crystal, and of beaded
jet,
Which one by one she in a river
threw,
Upon whose weeping margent she
was set;
Like usury, applying wet to wet,
Or monarch's hands that let not
bounty fall
Where want cries some, but where
excess begs all.

Of folded schedules had she many
a one,
Which she perused, sigh'd, tore,
and gave the flood;
Crack'd many a ring of posied gold
and bone
Bidding them find their sepulchres
in mud;
Found yet moe letters sadly penn'd

in blood,
With sleided silk feat and affectedly
Enswathed, and seal'd to curious
secrecy.

These often bathed she in her
fluxive eyes,
And often kiss'd, and often 'gan to
tear:
Cried 'O false blood, thou register
of lies,
What unapproved witness dost
thou bear!
Ink would have seem'd more black
and damned here!'
This said, in top of rage the lines
she rents,
Big discontent so breaking their
contents.

A reverend man that grazed his
cattle nigh--
Sometime a blusterer, that the
ruffle knew
Of court, of city, and had let go by

The swiftest hours, observed as
they flew--
Towards this afflicted fancy fastly
drew,
And, privileged by age, desires to
know
In brief the grounds and motives of
her woe.

So slides he down upon his
grained bat,
And comely-distant sits he by her
side;
When he again desires her, being
sat,
Her grievance with his hearing to
divide:
If that from him there may be aught
applied
Which may her suffering ecstasy
assuage,
'Tis promised in the charity of age.

'Father,' she says, 'though in me
you behold

The injury of many a blasting hour,
Let it not tell your judgment I am
old;
Not age, but sorrow, over me hath
power:
I might as yet have been a
spreading flower,
Fresh to myself, If I had self-
applied
Love to myself and to no love
beside.

'But, woe is me! too early I
attended
A youthful suit--it was to gain my
grace--
Of one by nature's outwards so
commended,
That maidens' eyes stuck over all
his face:
Love lack'd a dwelling, and made
him her place;
And when in his fair parts she did
abide,
She was new lodged and newly

deified.

'His browny locks did hang in
crooked curls;
And every light occasion of the
wind
Upon his lips their silken parcels
hurls.
What's sweet to do, to do will aptly
find:
Each eye that saw him did enchant
the mind,
For on his visage was in little
drawn
What largeness thinks in Paradise
was sawn.

'Small show of man was yet upon
his chin;
His phoenix down began but to
appear
Like unshorn velvet on that
termless skin
Whose bare out-bragg'd the web it
seem'd to wear:

Yet show'd his visage by that cost
more dear;
And nice affections wavering stood
in doubt
If best were as it was, or best
without.

'His qualities were beauteous as
his form,
For maiden-tongued he was, and
thereof free;
Yet, if men moved him, was he
such a storm
As oft 'twixt May and April is to see,
When winds breathe sweet, untidy
though they be.
His rudeness so with his authorized
youth
Did livery falseness in a pride of
truth.

'Well could he ride, and often men
would say
'That horse his mettle from his rider
takes:

Proud of subjection, noble by the
sway,
What rounds, what bounds, what
course, what stop
he makes!'
And controversy hence a question
takes,
Whether the horse by him became
his deed,
Or he his manage by the well-doing
steed.

'But quickly on this side the verdict
went:
His real habitude gave life and
grace
To appertainings and to ornament,
Accomplish'd in himself, not in his
case:
All aids, themselves made fairer by
their place,
Came for additions; yet their
purposed trim
Pieced not his grace, but were all
graced by him.

'So on the tip of his subduing
tongue
All kinds of arguments and
question deep,
All replication prompt, and reason
strong,
For his advantage still did wake
and sleep:
To make the weeper laugh, the
laugher weep,
He had the dialect and different
skill,
Catching all passions in his craft of
will:

'That he did in the general bosom
reign
Of young, of old; and sexes both
enchanted,
To dwell with him in thoughts, or to
remain
In personal duty, following where
he haunted:
Consents bewitch'd, ere he desire,

have granted;
And dialogued for him what he
would say,
Ask'd their own wills, and made
their wills obey.

'Many there were that did his
picture get,
To serve their eyes, and in it put
their mind;
Like fools that in th' imagination set
The goodly objects which abroad
they find
Of lands and mansions, theirs in
thought assign'd;
And labouring in moe pleasures to
bestow them
Than the true gouty landlord which
doth owe them:

'So many have, that never touch'd
his hand,
Sweetly supposed them mistress of
his heart.
My woeful self, that did in freedom

stand,
And was my own fee-simple, not in
part,
What with his art in youth, and
youth in art,
Threw my affections in his charmed
power,
Reserved the stalk and gave him
all my flower.

'Yet did I not, as some my equals
did,
Demand of him, nor being desired
yielded;
Finding myself in honour so forbid,
With safest distance I mine honour
shielded:
Experience for me many bulwarks
builded
Of proofs new-bleeding, which
remain'd the foil
Of this false jewel, and his
amorous spoil.

'But, ah, who ever shunn'd by

precedent
The destined ill she must herself
assay?
Or forced examples, 'gainst her
own content,
To put the by-past perils in her
way?
Counsel may stop awhile what will
not stay;
For when we rage, advice is often
seen
By blunting us to make our wits
more keen.

'Nor gives it satisfaction to our
blood,
That we must curb it upon others'
proof;
To be forbod the sweets that seem
so good,
For fear of harms that preach in our
behoof.
O appetite, from judgment stand
aloof!
The one a palate hath that needs

will taste,
Though Reason weep, and cry, 'It
is thy last.'

'For further I could say 'This man's
untrue,'
And knew the patterns of his foul
beguiling;
Heard where his plants in others'
orchards grew,
Saw how deceits were gilded in his
smiling;
Knew vows were ever brokers to
defiling;
Thought characters and words
merely but art,
And bastards of his foul adulterate
heart.

'And long upon these terms I held
my city,
Till thus he gan besiege me: 'Gentle maid,
Have of my suffering youth some
feeling pity,

And be not of my holy vows afraid:
That's to ye sworn to none was
ever said;
For feasts of love I have been call'd
unto,
Till now did ne'er invite, nor never
woo.

"All my offences that abroad you
see
Are errors of the blood, none of the
mind;
Love made them not: with acture
they may be,
Where neither party is nor true nor
kind:
They sought their shame that so
their shame did find;
And so much less of shame in me
remains,
By how much of me their reproach
contains.

"Among the many that mine eyes
have seen,

Not one whose flame my heart so
much as warm'd,
Or my affection put to the smallest
teen,
Or any of my leisures ever
charm'd:
Harm have I done to them, but
ne'er was harm'd;
Kept hearts in liveries, but mine
own was free,
And reign'd, commanding in his
monarchy.

"Look here, what tributes wounded
fancies sent me,
Of paled pearls and rubies red as
blood;
Figuring that they their passions
likewise lent me
Of grief and blushes, aptly
understood
In bloodless white and the
encrimson'd mood;
Effects of terror and dear modesty,
Encamp'd in hearts, but fighting

outwardly.

"And, lo, behold these talents of
their hair,
With twisted metal amorously
impleach'd,
I have received from many a
several fair,
Their kind acceptance weepingly
beseech'd,
With the annexions of fair gems
enrich'd,
And deep-brain'd sonnets that did
amplify
Each stone's dear nature, worth,
and quality.

"The diamond,--why, 'twas
beautiful and hard,
Whereto his invised properties did
tend;
The deep-green emerald, in whose
fresh regard
Weak sights their sickly radiance
do amend;

The heaven-hued sapphire and the
opal blend
With objects manifold: each several
stone,
With wit well blazon'd, smiled or
made some moan.

"Lo, all these trophies of affections
hot,
Of pensived and subdued desires
the tender,
Nature hath charged me that I
hoard them not,
But yield them up where I myself
must render,
That is, to you, my origin and
ender;
For these, of force, must your
oblations be,
Since I their altar, you enpatron
me.

"O, then, advance of yours that
phraseless hand,
Whose white weighs down the airy

scale of praise;
Take all these similes to your own
command,
Hallow'd with sighs that burning
lungs did raise;
What me your minister, for you
obeys,
Works under you; and to your audit
comes
Their distract parcels in combined
sums.

"Lo, this device was sent me from
a nun,
Or sister sanctified, of holiest note;
Which late her noble suit in court
did shun,
Whose rarest havings made the
blossoms dote;
For she was sought by spirits of
richest coat,
But kept cold distance, and did
thence remove,
To spend her living in eternal love.

"But, O my sweet, what labour is't
to leave
The thing we have not, mastering
what not strives,
Playing the place which did no form
receive,
Playing patient sports in
unconstrained gyves?
She that her fame so to herself
contrives,
The scars of battle 'scapeth by the
flight,
And makes her absence valiant,
not her might.

"O, pardon me, in that my boast is
true:
The accident which brought me to
her eye
Upon the moment did her force
subdue,
And now she would the caged
cloister fly:
Religious love put out Religion's
eye:

Not to be tempted, would she be
immured,
And now, to tempt, all liberty
procured.

"How mighty then you are, O, hear
me tell!
The broken bosoms that to me
belong
Have emptied all their fountains in
my well,
And mine I pour your ocean all
among:
I strong o'er them, and you o'er me
being strong,
Must for your victory us all congest,
As compound love to physic your
cold breast.

"My parts had power to charm a
sacred nun,
Who, disciplined, ay, dieted in
grace,
Believed her eyes when they to
assail begun,

All vows and consecrations giving
place:
O most potential love! vow, bond,
nor space,
In thee hath neither sting, knot, nor
confine,
For thou art all, and all things else
are thine.

"When thou impressest, what are
precepts worth
Of stale example? When thou wilt
inflame,
How coldly those impediments
stand forth
Of wealth, of filial fear, law,
kindred, fame!
Love's arms are peace, 'gainst rule,
'gainst sense,
'gainst shame,
And sweetens, in the suffering
pangs it bears,
The aloes of all forces, shocks, and
fears.

"Now all these hearts that do on
mine depend,
Feeling it break, with bleeding
groans they pine;
And supplicant their sighs to you
extend,
To leave the battery that you make
'gainst mine,
Lending soft audience to my sweet
design,
And credent soul to that strong-
bonded oath
That shall prefer and undertake my
troth.'

'This said, his watery eyes he did
dismount,
Whose sights till then were levell'd
on my face;
Each cheek a river running from a
fount
With brinish current downward
flow'd apace:
O, how the channel to the stream
gave grace!

Who glazed with crystal gate the
glowing roses
That flame through water which
their hue encloses.

'O father, what a hell of witchcraft
lies
In the small orb of one particular
tear!
But with the inundation of the eyes
What rocky heart to water will not
wear?
What breast so cold that is not
warmed here?
O cleft effect! cold modesty, hot
wrath,
Both fire from hence and chill
extincture hath.

'For, lo, his passion, but an art of
craft,
Even there resolved my reason into
tears;
There my white stole of chastity I
daff'd,

Shook off my sober guards and
civil fears;
Appear to him, as he to me
appears,
All melting; though our drops this
difference bore,
His poison'd me, and mine did him
restore.

'In him a plenitude of subtle matter,
Applied to cautels, all strange
forms receives,
Of burning blushes, or of weeping
water,
Or swooning paleness; and he
takes and leaves,
In either's aptness, as it best
deceives,
To blush at speeches rank to weep
at woes,
Or to turn white and swoon at
tragic shows.

'That not a heart which in his level
came

Could 'scape the hail of his all-
hurting aim,
Showing fair nature is both kind
and tame;
And, veil'd in them, did win whom
he would maim:
Against the thing he sought he
would exclaim;
When he most burn'd in heart-
wish'd luxury,
He preach'd pure maid, and
praised cold chastity.

'Thus merely with the garment of a
Grace
The naked and concealed fiend he
cover'd;
That th' unexperient gave the
tempter place,
Which like a cherubin above them
hover'd.
Who, young and simple, would not
be so lover'd?
Ay me! I fell; and yet do question
make

What I should do again for such a
sake.

'O, that infected moisture of his
eye,
O, that false fire which in his cheek
so glow'd,
O, that forced thunder from his
heart did fly,
O, that sad breath his spongy lungs
bestow'd,
O, all that borrow'd motion seeming
owed,
Would yet again betray the fore-
betray'd,
And new pervert a reconciled
maid!'

William Shakespeare

All the World's a Stage

All the world's a stage,
And all the men and women merely
players;
They have their exits and their
entrances,
And one man in his time plays
many parts,
His acts being seven ages. At first,
the infant,
Mewling and puking in the nurse's
arms.
Then the whining schoolboy, with
his satchel
And shining morning face, creeping
like snail
Unwillingly to school. And then the
lover,
Sighing like furnace, with a woeful
ballad
Made to his mistress' eyebrow.
Then a soldier,
Full of strange oaths and bearded
like the pard,

Jealous in honor, sudden and quick
in quarrel,
Seeking the bubble reputation
Even in the cannon's mouth. And
then the justice,
In fair round belly with good capon
lined,
With eyes severe and beard of
formal cut,
Full of wise saws and modern
instances;
And so he plays his part. The sixth
age shifts
Into the lean and slippered
pantaloon,
With spectacles on nose and
pouch on side;
His youthful hose, well saved, a
world too wide
For his shrunk shank, and his big
manly voice,
Turning again toward childish
treble, pipes
And whistles in his sound. Last
scene of all,

That ends this strange eventful
history,
Is second childishness and mere
oblivion,
Sans teeth, sans eyes, sans taste,
sans everything.

William Shakespeare

Blow, Blow, Thou Winter Wind

Blow, blow, thou winter wind
Thou art not so unkind
As man's ingratitude;
Thy tooth is not so keen,
Because thou art not seen,
Although thy breath be rude.

Heigh-ho! sing, heigh-ho! unto the
green holly:
Most freindship if feigning, most
loving mere folly:
Then heigh-ho, the holly!
This life is most jolly.

Freeze, freeze thou bitter sky,
That does not bite so nigh
As benefits forgot:
Though thou the waters warp,
Thy sting is not so sharp
As a friend remembered not.
Heigh-ho! sing, heigh-ho! unto the
green holly:
Most friendship is feigning, most

loving mere folly:
Then heigh-ho, the holly!
This life is most jolly.

William Shakespeare

Carpe Diem

O mistress mine, where are you
roaming?
O stay and hear! your true-love's
coming
That can sing both high and low;
Trip no further, pretty sweeting,
Journey's end in lovers' meeting--
Every wise man's son doth know.

What is love? 'tis not hereafter;
Present mirth hath present
laughter;
What's to come is still unsure:
In delay there lies no plenty,--
Then come kiss me, Sweet and
twenty,
Youth's a stuff will not endure.

William Shakespeare

Dirge of the Three Queens

URNS and odours bring away!
Vapours, sighs, darken the day!
Our dole more deadly looks than
dying;
Balms and gums and heavy
cheers,
Sacred vials fill'd with tears,
And clamours through the wild air
flying!

Come, all sad and solemn
shows,
That are quick-eyed Pleasure's
foes!
We convent naught else but
woes.

William Shakespeare

Fear No More

Fear no more the heat o' the sun;
Nor the furious winter's rages,
Thou thy worldly task hast done,
Home art gone, and ta'en thy
wages;
Golden lads and girls all must,
As chimney sweepers come to
dust.

Fear no more the frown of the
great,
Thou art past the tyrant's stroke:
Care no more to clothe and eat;
To thee the reed is as the oak:
The sceptre, learning, physic, must
All follow this, and come to dust.

Fear no more the lightning-flash,
Nor the all-dread thunder-stone;
Fear not slander, censure rash;
Thou hast finished joy and moan;
All lovers young, all lovers must
Consign to thee, and come to dust.

No exorciser harm thee!
Nor no witchcraft charm thee!
Ghost unlaid forbear thee!
Nothing ill come near thee!
Quiet consummation have;
And renowned be thy grave!

William Shakespeare

Fidele

FEAR no more the heat o' the sun,
Nor the furious winter's rages;
Thou thy worldly task hast done,
Home art gone, and ta'en thy
wages:
Golden lads and girls all must,
As chimney-sweepers, come to
dust.

Fear no more the frown o' the
great,
Thou art past the tyrant's stroke;
Care no more to clothe and eat;
To thee the reed is as the oak:
The sceptre, learning, physic, must
All follow this, and come to dust.

Fear no more the lightning-flash,
Nor the all-dreaded thunder-
stone;
Fear not slander, censure rash;
Thou hast finish'd joy and moan:
All lovers young, all lovers must

Consign to thee, and come to dust.

No exorciser harm thee!
Nor no witchcraft charm thee!
Ghost unlaid forbear thee!
Nothing ill come near thee!
Quiet consummation have;
And renowned be thy grave!

William Shakespeare

from Venus and Adonis

But, lo! from forth a copse that
neighbours by,
A breeding jennet, lusty, young,
and proud,
Adonis' trampling courser doth
espy,
And forth she rushes, snorts and
neighs aloud;
The strong-neck'd steed, being tied
unto a tree,
Breaketh his rein, and to her
straight goes he.

Imperiously he leaps, he neighs, he
bounds,
And now his woven girths he
breaks asunder;
The bearing earth with his hard
hoof he wounds,
Whose hollow womb resounds like
heaven's thunder;
The iron bit he crushes 'tween his
teeth

Controlling what he was controlled
with.

His ears up-prick'd; his braided
hanging mane
Upon his compass'd crest now
stand on end;
His nostrils drink the air, and forth
again,
As from a furnace, vapours doth he
send:
His eye, which scornfully glisters
like fire,
Shows his hot courage and his
high desire.

Sometime her trots, as if he told
the steps,
With gentle majesty and modest
pride;
Anon he rears upright, curvets and
leaps,
As who should say, 'Lo! thus my
strength is tried;
And this I do to captivate the eye

Of the fair breeder that is standing
by.'

What recketh he his rider's angry
stir,
His flattering 'Holla,' or his 'Stand, I
say?'
What cares he now for curb of
pricking spur?
For rich caparisons or trapping
gay?
He sees his love, and nothing else
he sees,
Nor nothing else with his proud
sight agrees.

Look, when a painter would
surpass the life,
In limning out a well-proportion'd
steed,
His art with nature's workmanship
at strife,
As if the dead the living should
exceed;
So did this horse excel a common

one,
In shape, in courage, colour, pace
and bone

Round-hoof'd, short-jointed,
fetlocks shag and long,
Broad breast, full eye, small head,
and nostril wide,
High crest, short ears, straight legs
and passing strong,
Thin mane, thick tail, broad
buttock, tender hide:
Look, what a horse should have he
did not lack,
Save a proud rider on so proud a
back.

Sometimes he scuds far off, and
there he stares;
Anon he starts at stirring of a
feather;
To bid the wind a race he now
prepares,
And whe'r he run or fly they know
not whether;

For through his mane and tail the
high wind sings,
Fanning the hairs, who wave like
feather'd wings.

He looks upon his love, and neighs
unto her;
She answers him as if she knew
his mind;
Being proud, as females are, to
see him woo her,
She puts on outward strangeness,
seems unkind,
Spurns at his love and scorns the
heat he feels,
Beating his kind embracements
with her heels.

Then, like a melancholy
malcontent,
He vails his tail that, like a falling
plume
Cool shadow to his melting buttock
lent:
He stamps, and bites the poor flies

in his fume.
His love, perceiving how he is
enrag'd,
Grew kinder, and his fury was
assuag'd.

His testy master goeth about to
take him;
When lo! the unback'd breeder, full
of fear,
Jealous of catching, swiftly doth
forsake him,
With her the horse, and left Adonis
there.
As they were mad, unto the wood
they hie them,
Out-stripping crows that strive to
over-fly them.

I prophesy they death, my living
sorrow,
If thou encounter with the boar to-
morrow.

"But if thou needs wilt hunt, be rul'd

by me;
Uncouple at the timorous flying
hare,
Or at the fox which lives by
subtlety,
Or at the roe which no encounter
dare:
Pursue these fearful creatures o'er
the downs,
And on they well-breath'd horse
keep with they hounds.

"And when thou hast on food the
purblind hare,
Mark the poor wretch, to overshoot
his troubles
How he outruns with winds, and
with what care
He cranks and crosses with a
thousand doubles:
The many musits through the
which he goes
Are like a labyrinth to amaze his
foes.

"Sometime he runs among a flock
of sheep,
To make the cunning hounds
mistake their smell,
And sometime where earth-delving
conies keep,
To stop the loud pursuers in their
yell,
And sometime sorteth with a herd
of deer;
Danger deviseth shifts; wit waits on
fear:

"For there his smell with other
being mingled,
The hot scent-snuffing hounds are
driven to doubt,
Ceasing their clamorous cry till
they have singled
With much ado the cold fault
cleanly out;
Then do they spend their mouths:
Echo replies,
As if another chase were in the
skies.

"By this, poor Wat, far off upon a
hill,
Stands on his hinder legs with
listening ear,
To hearken if his foes pursue him
still:
Anon their loud alarums he doth
hear;
And now his grief may be
compared well
To one sore sick that hears the
passing-bell.

"Then shalt thou see the dew-
bedabbled wretch
Turn, and return, indenting with the
way;
Each envious briar his weary legs
doth scratch,
Each shadow makes him stop,
each murmur stay:
For misery is trodden on by many,
And being low never reliev'd by
any.

"Lie quietly, and hear a little more;
Nay, do not struggle, for thou shalt
not rise:
To make thee hate the hunting of
the boar,
Unlike myself thou hear'st me
moralize,
Applying this to that, and so to so;
For love can comment upon every
woe."

William Shakespeare

From you have I been absent in the spring... (Sonnet 98)

From you have I been absent in the
spring,
When proud-pied April, dressed in
all his trim,
Hath put a spirit of youth in
everything,
That heavy Saturn laughed and
leaped with him,
Yet nor the lays of birds, nor the
sweet smell
Of different flowers in odor and in
hue,
Could make me any summer's
story tell,
Or from their proud lap pluck them
where they grew.
Nor did I wonder at the lily's white,
Nor praise the deep vermilion in
the rose;
They were but sweet, but figures of
delight,
Drawn after you, you pattern of all

those.
Yet seemed it winter still, and, you away,
As with your shadow I with these did play.

William Shakespeare

Full Fathom Five

Full fathom five thy father lies;
Of his bones are coral made;
Those are pearls that were his
eyes:
Nothing of him that doth fade
But doth suffer a sea-change
Into something rich and strange.
Sea-nymphs hourly ring his knell:
Ding-dong.
Hark! now I hear them,--ding-dong,
bell.

William Shakespeare

Hark! Hark! The Lark

Hark! hark! the lark at heaven's
gate sings,
And Phoebus 'gins arise,
His steeds to water at those
springs
On chalic'd flowers that lies;
And winking Mary-buds begin
To ope their golden eyes;
With everything that pretty is,
My lady sweet, arise:
Arise, arise!

William Shakespeare

How Like A Winter Hath My Absence Been

How like a winter hath my absence
been
From Thee, the pleasure of the
fleeting year!
What freezings have I felt; what
dark days seen,
What old December's bareness
everywhere!

And yet this time removed was
summer's time:
The teeming autumn big with rich
increase,
Bearing the wanton burden of the
prime
Like widow'd wombs after their
lords' decease;

Yet this abundant issue seem'd to
me
But hope of orphans, and
unfather'd fruit;

For summer and his pleasures wait
on thee,
And, thou away, the very birds are
more;
Or if they sing, 'tis with so dull a
cheer,
That leaves look pale, dreading the
winter's near.

William Shakespeare

It was a Lover and his Lass

IT was a lover and his lass,
With a hey, and a ho, and a hey
nonino,
That o'er the green corn-field did
pass,
In the spring time, the only pretty
ring time,
When birds do sing, hey ding a
ding, ding;
Sweet lovers love the spring.

Between the acres of the rye,
With a hey, and a ho, and a hey
nonino,
These pretty country folks would
lie,
In the spring time, the only pretty
ring time,
When birds do sing, hey ding a
ding, ding;
Sweet lovers love the spring.

This carol they began that hour,

With a hey, and a ho, and a hey
nonino,
How that life was but a flower
In the spring time, the only pretty
ring time,
When birds do sing, hey ding a
ding, ding;
Sweet lovers love the spring.

And, therefore, take the present
time
With a hey, and a ho, and a hey
nonino,
For love is crown`d with the prime
In the spring time, the only pretty
ring time,
When birds do sing, hey ding a
ding, ding;
Sweet lovers love the spring.

William Shakespeare

Juliet's Soliloquy

Farewell!--God knows when we
shall meet again.
I have a faint cold fear thrills
through my veins
That almost freezes up the heat of
life:
I'll call them back again to comfort
me;--
Nurse!--What should she do here?
My dismal scene I needs must act
alone.--
Come, vial.--
What if this mixture do not work at
all?
Shall I be married, then, to-morrow
morning?--
No, No!--this shall forbid it:--lie thou
there.--
What if it be a poison, which the
friar
Subtly hath minister'd to have me
dead,
Lest in this marriage he should be

dishonour'd,
Because he married me before to
Romeo?
I fear it is: and yet methinks it
should not,
For he hath still been tried a holy
man:--
I will not entertain so bad a
thought.--
How if, when I am laid into the
tomb,
I wake before the time that Romeo
Come to redeem me? there's a
fearful point!
Shall I not then be stifled in the
vault,
To whose foul mouth no
healthsome air breathes in,
And there die strangled ere my
Romeo comes?
Or, if I live, is it not very like
The horrible conceit of death and
night,
Together with the terror of the
place,--

As in a vault, an ancient
receptacle,
Where, for this many hundred
years, the bones
Of all my buried ancestors are
pack'd;
Where bloody Tybalt, yet but green
in earth,
Lies festering in his shroud; where,
as they say,
At some hours in the night spirits
resort;--
Alack, alack, is it not like that I,
So early waking,--what with
loathsome smells,
And shrieks like mandrakes torn
out of the earth,
That living mortals, hearing them,
run mad;--
O, if I wake, shall I not be
distraught,
Environed with all these hideous
fears?
And madly play with my
forefathers' joints?

And pluck the mangled Tybalt from his shroud?
And, in this rage, with some great kinsman's bone,
As with a club, dash out my desperate brains?--
O, look! methinks I see my cousin's ghost
Seeking out Romeo, that did spit his body
Upon a rapier's point:--stay, Tybalt, stay!--
Romeo, I come! this do I drink to thee.

William Shakespeare

Love

TELL me where is Fancy bred,
Or in the heart or in the head?
How begot, how nourished?
Reply, reply.
It is engender'd in the eyes,
With gazing fed; and Fancy dies
In the cradle where it lies.
Let us all ring Fancy's knell:
I'll begin it,--Ding, dong, bell.
All. Ding, dong, bell.

William Shakespeare

Now, my co-mates and brothers in exile

Now, my co-mates and brothers in
exile,
Hath not old customs make this life
more sweet
Than that of painted pomp? Are not
these woods
More free from peril than the
envious court!
Here feel we not the penalty of
Adam,
The seasons difference; as the icy
fang
And churlish chiding of the winters
wind,
Which when it bites and blows
upon my body,
Even till I shrink with cold, I smile
and say
This is no flattery; these are
counsellors
That feelingly persuade me what I
am.

Sweet are the uses of adversity;
Which, like the toad, ugly and
venomous,
Wears yet a precious jewel in his
head;
And this our life, exempt from
public haunt,
Finds tongues in trees, books in
the running brooks,
Sermons in stones, and good in
everything.
I would not change it.

William Shakespeare

O Never Say That I Was False of Heart

O never say that I was false of
heart,
Though absence seem'd my flame
to qualify:
As easy might I from myself depart
As from my soul, which in thy
breast doth lie;

That is my home of love; if I have
ranged,
Like him that travels, I return again,
Just to the time, not with the time
exchanged,
So that myself bring water for my
stain.

Never believe, though in my nature
reign'd
All frailties that besiege all kinds of
blood,
That it could so preposterously be
stain'd

To leave for nothing all thy sum of
good:

For nothing this wide universe I
call,
Save thou, my rose: in it thou art
my all.

William Shakespeare

Orpheus

? or John Fletcher.

ORPHEUS with his lute made trees
And the mountain tops that freeze
Bow themselves when he did
sing:
To his music plants and flowers
Ever sprung; as sun and showers
There had made a lasting spring.

Every thing that heard him play,
Even the billows of the sea,
Hung their heads and then lay
by.
In sweet music is such art,
Killing care and grief of heart
Fall asleep, or hearing, die.

William Shakespeare

Shall I compare thee to a summer's day? (Sonnet 18)

Shall I compare thee to a summer's
day?
Thou art more lovely and more
temperate.
Rough winds do shake the darling
buds of May,
And summer's lease hath all too
short a date.
Sometime too hot the eye of
heaven shines,
And often is his gold complexion
dimmed;
And every fair from fair sometime
declines,
By chance, or nature's changing
course, untrimmed;
But thy eternal summer shall not
fade,
Nor lose possession of that fair
thou ow'st,
Nor shall death brag thou
wand'rest in his shade,

When in eternal lines to Time thou grow'st.
So long as men can breathe, or eyes can see,
So long lives this, and this gives life to thee.

William Shakespeare

Sigh No More

Sigh no more, ladies, sigh no more,
Men were deceivers ever;
One foot in sea, and one on shore,
To one thing constant never.
Then sigh not so,
But let them go,
And be you blith and bonny,
Converting all your sounds of woe
Into Hey nonny, nonny.

Sing no more ditties, sing no mo
Of dumps so dull and heavy;
The fraud of men was ever so,
Since summer first was leavy.
Then sigh not so,
But let them go,
And be you blith and bonny,
Converting all your sounds of woe
Into Hey nonny, nonny.

William Shakespeare

Silvia

WHO is Silvia? What is she?
That all our swains commend
her?
Holy, fair, and wise is she;
The heaven such grace did lend
her,
That she might admired be.

Is she kind as she is fair?
For beauty lives with kindness:
Love doth to her eyes repair,
To help him of his blindness;
And, being help'd, inhabits there.

Then to Silvia let us sing,
That Silvia is excelling;
She excels each mortal thing
Upon the dull earth dwelling:
To her let us garlands bring.

William Shakespeare

Sonnet LIV

O, how much more doth beauty
beauteous seem
By that sweet ornament which truth
doth give!
The rose looks fair, but fairer we it
deem
For that sweet odour which doth in
it live.
The canker-blooms have full as
deep a dye
As the perfumed tincture of the
roses,
Hang on such thorns and play as
wantonly
When summer's breath their
masked buds discloses:
But, for their virtue only is their
show,
They live unwoo'd and unrespected
fade,
Die to themselves. Sweet roses do
not so;
Of their sweet deaths are sweetest

odours made:
And so of you, beauteous and
lovely youth,
When that shall fade, my verse
distills your truth.

William Shakespeare

Sonnet 1

From fairest creatures we desire
increase,
That thereby beauty's rose might
never die,
But as the riper should by time
decease,
His tender heir might bear his
memory:
But thou, contracted to thine own
bright eyes,
Feed'st thy light'st flame with self-
substantial fuel,
Making a famine where abundance
lies,
Thyself thy foe, to thy sweet self
too cruel.
Thou that art now the world's fresh
ornament
And only herald to the gaudy
spring,
Within thine own bud buriest thy
content
And, tender churl, makest waste in

niggarding.
Pity the world, or else this glutton
be,
To eat the world's due, by the
grave and thee.

William Shakespeare

Sonnet 10

For shame, deny that thou bear'st
love to any
Who for thy self art so unprovident.
Grant, if thou wilt, thou art beloved
of many,
But that thou none lov'st is most
evident;
For thou art so possessed with
murd'rous hate,
That 'gainst thy self thou stick'st not
to conspire,
Seeking that beauteous roof to
ruinate
Which to repair should be thy chief
desire.
O, change thy thought, that I may
change my mind!
Shall hate be fairer lodged than
gentle love?
Be as thy presence is gracious and
kind,
Or to thy self at least kind-hearted
prove,

Make thee another self, for love of
me,
That beauty still may live in thine or
thee.

William Shakespeare

Sonnet 100

Where art thou, Muse, that thou
forget'st so long
To speak of that which gives thee
all thy might?
Spend'st thou thy fury on some
worthless song,
Darkening thy power to lend base
subjects light?
Return, forgetful Muse, and straight
redeem
In gentle numbers time so idly
spent;
Sing to the ear that doth thy lays
esteem,
And gives thy pen both skill and
argument.
Rise, resty Muse, my love's sweet
face survey
If time have any wrinkle graven
there;
If any, be a satire to decay,
And make time's spoils despisèd
everywhere.

Give my love fame faster than
Time wastes life;
So thou prevent'st his scythe and
crooked knife.

William Shakespeare

Sonnet 101

O truant Muse, what shall be thy
amends
For thy neglect of truth in beauty
dyed?
Both truth and beauty on my love
depends;
So dost thou too, and therein
dignified.
Make answer, Muse. Wilt thou not
haply say,
"Truth needs no colour with his
colour fixed,
Beauty no pencil, beauty's truth to
lay,
But best is best, if never
intermixed"?
Because he needs no praise, wilt
thou be dumb?
Excuse not silence so, for't lies in
thee
To make him much outlive a gilded
tomb
And to be praised of ages yet to

be.
Then do thy office, Muse; I teach
thee how
To make him seem, long hence, as
he shows now.

William Shakespeare

Sonnet 102

My love is strengthened, though
more weak in seeming;
I love not less, though less the
show appear;
That love is merchandized, whose
rich esteeming
The owner's tongue doth publish
everywhere.
Our love was new, and then but in
the spring
When I was wont to greet it with my
lays,
As Philomel in summer's front doth
sing,
And stops her pipe in growth of
riper days—
Not that the summer is less
pleasant now
Than when her mournful hymns did
hush the night,
But that wild music burthens every
bough,
And sweets grown common lose

their dear delight.
Therefore like her I sometime hold
my tongue,
Because I would not dull you with
my song.

William Shakespeare

Sonnet 103

Alack, what poverty my Muse
brings forth,
That having such a scope to show
her pride,
The argument all bare is of more
worth
Than when it hath my added praise
beside.
O, blame me not if I no more can
write!
Look in your glass, and there
appears a face
That overgoes my blunt invention
quite,
Dulling my lines, and doing me
disgrace.
Were it not sinful then striving to
mend,
To mar the subject that before was
well?
For to no other pass my verses
tend
Than of your graces and your gifts

to tell;
And more, much more than in my
verse can sit,
Your own glass shows you when
you look in it.

William Shakespeare

Sonnet 104

To me, fair friend, you never can
be old,
For as you were when first your
eye I ey'd,
Such seems your beauty still.
Three winters cold,
Have from the forests shook three
summers' pride,
Three beauteous springs to yellow
autumn turn'd,
In process of the seasons have I
seen,
Three April perfumes in three hot
Junes burn'd,
Since first I saw you fresh, which
yet are green.
Ah! yet doth beauty like a dial-
hand,
Steal from his figure, and no pace
perceiv'd;
So your sweet hue, which methinks

still doth stand,
Hath motion, and mine eye may be

deceiv'd:
For fear of which, hear this thou
age unbred:
Ere you were born was beauty's
summer dead.

William Shakespeare

Sonnet 105

Let not my love be called idolatry,
Nor my belovèd as an idol show,
Since all alike my songs and
praises be
To one, of one, still such, and ever
so.
Kind is my love today, tomorrow
kind,
Still constant in a wondrous
excellence;
Therefore my verse to constancy
confined,
One thing expressing, leaves out
difference.
"Fair, kind, and true" is all my
argument,
"Fair, kind, and true" varying to
other words;
And in this change is my invention
spent,
Three themes in one, which
wondrous scope affords.
Fair, kind, and true, have often

lived alone.
Which three till now never kept
seat in one.

William Shakespeare

Sonnet 106

When in the chronicle of wasted
time
I see descriptions of the fairest
wights,
And beauty making beautiful old
rhyme
In praise of ladies dead, and lovely
knights,
Then, in the blazon of sweet
beauty's best,
Of hand, of foot, of lip, of eye, of
brow,
I see their antique pen would have
expressed
Even such a beauty as you master
now.
So all their praises are but
prophecies
Of this our time, all you prefiguring;
And, for they looked but with
divining eyes,
They had not skill enough your
worth to sing.

For we, which now behold these
present days,
Have eyes to wonder, but lack
tongues to praise.

William Shakespeare

Sonnet 107

Not mine own fears, nor the
prophetic soul
Of the wide world dreaming on
things to come,
Can yet the lease of my true love
control,
Suppos'd as forfeit to a confin'd
doom.
The mortal moon hath her eclipse
endur'd
And the sad augurs mock their own
presage;
Incertainties now crown
themselves assur'd
And peace proclaims olives of
endless age.
Now with the drops of this most
balmy time
My love looks fresh, and Death to
me subscribes,
Since, spite of him, I'll live in this
poor rhyme,
While he insults o'er dull and

speechless tribes;
And thou in this shalt find thy
monument,
When tyrants' crests and tombs of
brass are spent.

William Shakespeare

Sonnet 109

O, never say that I was false of
heart,
Though absence seemed my flame
to qualify.
As easy might I from my self depart
As from my soul which in thy breast
doth lie.
That is my home of love; if I have
ranged,
Like him that travels I return again,
Just to the time, not with the time
exchanged,
So that myself bring water for my
stain.
Never believe though in my nature
reigned
All frailties that besiege all kinds of
blood,
That it could so preposterously be
stained
To leave for nothing all thy sum of
good;
For nothing this wide universe I call

Save thou, my rose, in it thou art my all.

William Shakespeare

Sonnet 112

Your love and pity doth th'
impression fill
Which vulgar scandal stamped
upon my brow;
For what care I who calls me well
or ill,
So you o'ergreen my bad, my good
allow?
You are my all the world, and I
must strive
To know my shames and praises
from your tongue;
None else to me, nor I to none
alive,
That my steeled sense or changes,
right or wrong.
In so profound abysm I throw all
care
Of others' voices that my adder's
sense
To critic and to flatterer stoppèd
are.
Mark how with my neglect I do

dispense.
You are so strongly in my purpose
bred,
That all the world besides,
methinks, are dead.

William Shakespeare

Sonnet 11

As fast as thou shalt wane, so fast
thou grow'st
In one of thine, from that which
thou departest,
And that fresh blood which youngly
thou bestow'st,
Thou mayst call thine when thou
from youth convertest.
Herein lives wisdom, beauty, and
increase;
Without this folly, age, and cold
decay,
If all were minded so, the times
should cease,
And threescore year would make
the world away.
Let those whom Nature hath not
made for store,
Harsh, featureless, and rude,
barrenly perish;
Look whom she best endowed, she
gave the more,
Which bounteous gift thou shouldst

in bounty cherish.
She carved thee for her seal, and
meant thereby,
Thou shouldst print more, not let
that copy die.

William Shakespeare

Sonnet 113

Since I left you, mine eye is in my
mind,
And that which governs me to go
about
Doth part his function, and is partly
blind,
Seems seeing, but effectually is
out;
For it no form delivers to the heart
Of bird, of flower, or shape which it
doth latch;
Of his quick objects hath the mind
no part,
Nor his own vision holds what it
doth catch;
For if it see the rud'st or gentlest
sight,
The most sweet-favour or
deformed'st creature,
The mountain or the sea, the day
or night,
The crow or dove, it shapes them
to your feature.

Incapable of more, replete with you,
My most true mind thus maketh mine untrue.

William Shakespeare

Sonnet 114

Or whether doth my mind, being
crowned with you,
Drink up the monarch's plague, this
flattery?
Or whether shall I say mine eye
saith true,
And that your love taught it this
alchemy,
To make of monsters, and things
indigest,
Such cherubins as your sweet self
resemble,
Creating every bad a perfect best
As fast as objects to his beams
assemble?
O, 'tis the first, 'tis flattery in my
seeing,
And my great mind most kingly
drinks it up;
Mine eye well knows what with his
gust is 'greeing,
And to his palate doth prepare the
cup.

If it be poisoned, 'tis the lesser sin
That mine eye loves it and doth
first begin.

William Shakespeare

Sonnet 115

Those lines that I before have writ
do lie,
Even those that said I could not
love you dearer;
Yet then my judgment knew no
reason why
My most full flame should
afterwards burn clearer,
But reckoning Time, whose
millioned accidents
Creep in 'twixt vows, and change
decrees of kings,
Tan sacred beauty, blunt the
sharp'st intents,
Divert strong minds to the course
of alt'ring things—
Alas, why, fearing of Time's
tyranny,
Might I not then say, "Now I love
you best,"
When I was certain o'er incertainty,
Crowning the present, doubting of
the rest?

Love is a babe; then might I not
say so,
To give full growth to that which still
doth grow.

William Shakespeare

Sonnet 116

Let me not to the marriage of true
minds
Admit impediments. Love is not
love
Which alters when it alteration
finds,
Or bends with the remover to
remove.
O no, it is an ever-fixèd mark
That looks on tempests and is
never shaken;
It is the star to every wand'ring
bark,
Whose worth's unknown, although
his height be taken.
Love's not Time's fool, though rosy
lips and cheeks
Within his bending sickle's
compass come;
Love alters not with his brief hours
and weeks,
But bears it out even to the edge of
doom.

If this be error and upon me
proved,
I never writ, nor no man ever loved.

William Shakespeare

Sonnet 118

Like as to make our appetite more
keen
With eager compounds we our
palate urge,
As to prevent our maladies unseen,
We sicken to shun sickness when
we purge.
Even so being full of your ne'er-
cloying sweetness,
To bitter sauces did I frame my
feeding;
And, sick of welfare, found a kind
of meetness
To be diseased ere that there was
true needing.
Thus policy in love t' anticipate
The ills that were not, grew to faults
assured,
And brought to medicine a healthful
state
Which, rank of goodness, would by
ill be cured.
But thence I learn and find the

lesson true:
Drugs poison him that so fell sick of
you.

William Shakespeare

Sonnet 119

What potions have I drunk of Siren
tears,
Distilled from limbecks foul as hell
within,
Applying fears to hopes, and hopes
to fears,
Still losing when I saw my self to
win!
What wretched errors hath my
heart committed,
Whilst it hath thought it self so
blessèd never!
How have mine eyes out of their
spheres been fitted
In the distraction of this madding
fever!
O, benefit of ill, now I find true
That better is, by evil still made
better;
And ruined love, when it is built
anew,
Grows fairer than at first, more
strong, far greater.

So I return rebuked to my content,
And gain by ills thrice more than I
have spent.

William Shakespeare

Sonnet 120

That you were once unkind
befriends me now,
And for that sorrow, which I then
did feel,
Needs must I under my
transgression bow,
Unless my nerves were brass or
hammered steel.
For if you were by my unkindness
shaken
As I by yours, y'have passed a hell
of time,
And I, a tyrant, have no leisure
taken
To weigh how once I suffered in
your crime.
O, that our night of woe might have
remembered
My deepest sense how hard true
sorrow hits,
And soon to you, as you to me
then, tendered
The humble salve which wounded

bosoms fits!
But that your trespass now
becomes a fee;
Mine ransoms yours, and yours
must ransom me.

William Shakespeare

Sonnet 122

Thy gift, thy tables, are within my
brain
Full charactered with lasting
memory,
Which shall above that idle rank
remain,
Beyond all date, even to eternity:
Or, at the least, so long as brain
and heart
Have faculty by nature to subsist;
Till each to razed oblivion yield his
part
Of thee, thy record never can be
missed.
That poor retention could not so
much hold,
Nor need I tallies thy dear love to
score;
Therefore to give them from me
was I bold,
To trust those tables that receive
thee more:
To keep an adjunct to remember

thee
Were to import forgetfulness in me.

William Shakespeare

Sonnet 123

No, Time, thou shalt not boast that
I do change.
Thy pyramids built up with newer
might
To me are nothing novel, nothing
strange;
They are but dressings of a former
sight.
Our dates are brief, and therefore
we admire
What thou dost foist upon us that is
old,
And rather make them born to our
desire
Than think that we before have
heard them told.
Thy registers and thee I both defy,
Not wond'ring at the present, nor
the past,
For thy records, and what we see
doth lie,
Made more or less by thy continual
haste:

This I do vow and this shall ever
be:
I will be true despite thy scythe and
thee.

William Shakespeare

Sonnet 130

My mistress' eyes are nothing like
the sun;
Coral is far more red than her lips'
red;
If snow be white, why then her
breasts are dun;
If hairs be wires, black wires grow
on her head.
I have seen roses damasked, red
and white,
But no such roses see I in her
cheeks,
And in some perfumes is there
more delight
Than in the breath that from my
mistress reeks.
I love to hear her speak, yet well I
know,
That music hath a far more
pleasing sound.
I grant I never saw a goddess go;
My mistress when she walks treads
on the ground.

And yet, by heaven, I think my love as rare
As any she belied with false compare.

William Shakespeare

Sonnet 131

Thou art as tyrannous, so as thou
art,
As those whose beauties proudly
make them cruel;
For well thou know'st to my dear
doting heart
Thou art the fairest and most
precious jewel.
Yet, in good faith, some say that
thee behold
Thy face hath not the power to
make love groan;
To say they err I dare not be so
bold,
Although I swear it to myself alone.
And to be sure that is not false I
swear,
A thousand groans but thinking on
thy face,
One on another's neck do witness
bear
Thy black is fairest in my
judgment's place.

In nothing art thou black save in thy
deeds,
And thence this slander, as I think,
proceeds.

William Shakespeare

Sonnet 132

Thine eyes I love, and they, as
pitying me,
Knowing thy heart torment me with
disdain,
Have put on black, and loving
mourners be,
Looking with pretty ruth upon my
pain.
And truly not the morning sun of
heaven
Better becomes the grey cheeks of
the east,
Nor that full star that ushers in the
even
Doth half that glory to the sober
west
As those two mourning eyes
become thy face.
O, let it then as well beseem thy
heart
To mourn for me since mourning
doth thee grace,
And suit thy pity like in every part.

Then will I swear beauty herself is black,
And all they foul that thy complexion lack.

William Shakespeare

Sonnet 133

Beshrew that heart that makes my
heart to groan
For that deep wound it gives my
friend and me!
Is't not enough to torture me alone,
But slave to slavery my sweet'st
friend must be?
Me from my self thy cruel eye hath
taken,
And my next self thou harder hast
engrossed.
Of him, myself, and thee I am
forsaken—
A torment thrice threefold thus to
be crossed.
Prison my heart in thy steel
bosom's ward,
But then my friend's heart let my
poor heart bail;
Whoe'er keeps me, let my heart be
his guard,
Thou canst not then use rigour in
my jail.

And yet thou wilt; for I, being pent in thee,
Perforce am thine, and all that is in me.

William Shakespeare

Sonnet 134

So, now I have confessed that he
is thine,
And I my self am mortgaged to thy
will,
Myself I'll forfeit, so that other mine
Thou wilt restore to be my comfort
still.
But thou wilt not, nor he will not be
free,
For thou art covetous, and he is
kind,
He learned but surety-like to write
for me
Under that bond that him as fist
doth bind.
The statute of thy beauty thou wilt
take,
Thou usurer, that putt'st forth all to
use,
And sue a friend, came debtor for
my sake;
So him I lose through my unkind
abuse.

Him have I lost, thou hast both him
and me;
He pays the whole, and yet am I
not free.

William Shakespeare

Sonnet 135

Whoever hath her wish, thou hast
thy will,
And Will to boot, and Will in
overplus;
More than enough am I that vex
thee still,
To thy sweet will making addition
thus.
Wilt thou, whose will is large and
spacious,
Not once vouchsafe to hide my will
in thine?
Shall will in others seem right
gracious,
And in my will no fair acceptance
shine?
The sea, all water, yet receives rain
still,
And in abundance addeth to his
store;
So thou being rich in will add to thy
will
One will of mine to make thy large

will more.
Let no unkind, no fair beseechers
kill,
Think all but one, and me in that
one Will.

William Shakespeare

Sonnet 140

Be wise as thou art cruel; do not
press
My tongue-tied patience with too
much disdain,
Lest sorrow lend me words and
words express
The manner of my pity-wanting
pain.
If I might teach thee wit, better it
were,
Though not to love, yet, love, to tell
me so,
As testy sick men, when their
deaths be near,
No news but health from their
physicians know.
For if I should despair, I should
grow mad,
And in my madness might speak ill
of thee,
Now this ill-wresting world is grown
so bad,
Mad slanderers by mad ears

believèd be.
That I may not be so, nor thou
belied,
Bear thine eyes straight, though thy
proud heart go wide.

William Shakespeare

Sonnet 141

In faith, I do not love thee with mine
eyes,
For they in thee a thousand errors
note;
But 'tis my heart that loves what
they despise,
Who in despite of view is pleased
to dote.
Nor are mine cars with thy tongue's
tune delighted,
Nor tender feeling to base touches
prone,
Nor taste, nor smell, desire to be
invited
To any sensual feast with thee
alone;
But my five wits, nor my five
senses can
Dissuade one foolish heart from
serving thee,
Who leaves unswayed the likeness
of a man,
Thy proud heart's slave and vassal

wretch to be.
Only my plague thus far I count my
gain,
That she that makes me sin
awards me pain.

William Shakespeare

Sonnet 142

Love is my sin, and thy dear virtue
hate,
Hate of my sin, grounded on sinful
loving,
O, but with mine, compare thou
thine own state,
And thou shalt find it merits not
reproving,
Or if it do, not from those lips of
thine
That have profaned their scarlet
ornaments
And sealed false bonds of love as
oft as mine,
Robbed others' beds' revenues of
their rents.
Be it lawful I love thee as thou
lov'st those
Whom thine eyes woo as mine
importune thee.
Root pity in thy heart, that when it
grows
Thy pity may deserve to pitied be.

If thou dost seek to have what thou
dost hide,
By self-example mayst thou be
denied!

William Shakespeare

Sonnet 143

Lo, as a careful huswife runs to
catch
One of her feathered creatures
broke away,
Sets down her babe and makes all
swift dispatch
In pursuit of the thing she would
have stay,
Whilst her neglected child holds
her in chase,
Cries to catch her whose busy care
is bent
To follow that which flies before her
face,
Not prizing her poor infant's
discontent:
So runn'st thou after that which
flies from thee,
Whilst I, thy babe, chase thee afar
behind;
But if thou catch thy hope turn back
to me,
And play the mother's part: kiss

me, be kind.
So will I pray that thou mayst have
thy Will,
If thou turn back and my loud
crying still.

William Shakespeare

Sonnet 144

Two loves I have, of comfort and
despair,
Which like two spirits do suggest
me still:
The better angel is a man right fair,
The worser spirit a woman
coloured ill.
To win me soon to hell, my female
evil
Tempteth my better angel from my
side,
And would corrupt my saint to be a
devil,
Wooing his purity with her foul
pride.
And whether that my angel be
turned fiend,
Suspect I may, yet not directly tell;
But being both from me both to
each friend,
I guess one angel in another's hell.
Yet this shall I ne'er know, but live
in doubt,

Till my bad angel fire my good one out.

William Shakespeare

Sonnet 145

Those lips that Love's own hand
did make
Breathed forth the sound that said
"I hate"
To me that languished for her sake;
But when she saw my woeful state,
Straight in her heart did mercy
come,
Chiding that tongue that ever sweet
Was used in giving gentle doom,
And taught it thus anew to greet:
"I hate" she altered with an end,
That followed it as gentle day
Doth follow night, who like a fiend
From heaven to hell is flown away.
"I hate" from hate away she threw,
And saved my life, saying "not
you."

William Shakespeare

Sonnet 150

O, from what power hast thou this
powerful might
With insufficiency my heart to
sway?
To make me give the lie to my true
sight,
And swear that brightness doth not
grace the day?
Whence hast thou this becoming of
things ill,
That in the very refuse of thy deeds
There is such strength and
warrantise of skill
That, in my mind, thy worst all best
exceeds?
Who taught thee how to make me
love thee more,
The more I hear and see just cause
of hate?
O, though I love what others do
abhor,
With others thou shouldst not
abhor my state.

If thy unworthiness raised love in
me,
More worthy I to be beloved of
thee.

William Shakespeare

Sonnet 151

Love is too young to know what
conscience is;
Yet who knows not conscience is
born of love?
Then, gentle cheater, urge not my
amiss,
Lest guilty of my faults thy sweet
self prove.
For thou betraying me, I do betray
My nobler part to my gross body's
treason;
My soul doth tell my body that he
may
Triumph in love; flesh stays no
farther reason,
But, rising at thy name, doth point
out thee
As his triumphant prize. Proud of
this pride,
He is contented thy poor drudge to
be,
To stand in thy affairs, fall by thy
side.

No want of conscience hold it that I
call,
Her "love" for whose dear love I
rise and fall.

William Shakespeare

Sonnet 152

In loving thee thou know'st I am
forsworn,
But thou art twice forsworn to me
love swearing:
In act thy bed-vow broke and new
faith torn
In vowing new hate after new love
bearing.
But why of two oaths' breach do I
accuse thee,
When I break twenty? I am
perjured most,
For all my vows are oaths but to
misuse thee,
And all my honest faith in thee is
lost.
For I have sworn deep oaths of thy
deep kindness,
Oaths of thy love, thy truth, thy
constancy,
And to enlighten thee gave eyes to
blindness,
Or made them swear against the

thing they see.
For I have sworn thee fair. More
perjured eye,
To swear against the truth so foul a
lie!

William Shakespeare

Sonnet 153

Cupid laid by his brand and fell
asleep,
A maid of Dian's this advantage
found,
And his love-kindling fire did
quickly steep
In a cold valley-fountain of that
ground;
Which borrowed from this holy fire
of Love
A dateless lively heat still to
endure,
And grew a seeting bath, which yet
men prove
Against strange maladies a
sovereign cure.
But at my mistress' eye Love's
brand new-fired,
The boy for trial needs would touch
my breast;
I, sick withal, the help of bath
desired,
And thither hied a sad distempered

guest,
But found no cure. The bath for my
help lies
Where Cupid got new fire—my
mistress' eyes.

William Shakespeare

Sonnet 154

The little love god lying once
asleep
Laid by his side his heart-inflaming
brand,
Whilst many nymphs that vowed
chaste life to keep
Came tripping by; but in her
maiden hand,
The fairest votary took up that fire
Which many legions of true hearts
had warmed,
And so the general of hot desire
Was sleeping by a virgin hand
disarmed.
This brand she quenched in a cool
well by,
Which from Love's fire took heat
perpetual,
Growing a bath and healthful
remedy,
For men discased; but I, my
mistress' thrall,
Came there for cure and this by

that I prove,
Love's fire heats water, water cools
not love.

William Shakespeare

Spring

When daisies pied, and violets
blue,
And lady-smocks all silver-white,
And cuckoo-buds of yellow hue
Do paint the meadows with delight,
The cuckoo then, on every tree,
Mocks married men, for thus sings
he:
'Cuckoo!
Cuckoo, cuckoo!' O word of fear,
Unpleasing to a married ear.
When shepherds pipe on oaten
straws,
And merry larks are ploughmen's
clocks,
When turtles tread, and rooks, and
daws,
And maidens bleach their summer
smocks,
The cuckoo then, on every tree,
Mocks married men, for thus sings
he:
'Cuckoo!

Cuckoo, cuckoo!' O word of fear,
Unpleasing to a married ear.

William Shakespeare

Spring and Winter i

WHEN daisies pied and violets
blue,
And lady-smocks all silver-white,
And cuckoo-buds of yellow hue
Do paint the meadows with
delight,
The cuckoo then, on every tree,
Mocks married men; for thus sings
he,
Cuckoo!
Cuckoo, cuckoo!--O word of fear,
Unpleasing to a married ear!

When shepherds pipe on oaten
straws,
And merry larks are ploughmen's
clocks,
When turtles tread, and rooks, and
daws,
And maidens bleach their
summer smocks
The cuckoo then, on every tree,
Mocks married men; for thus sings

he,
Cuckoo!
Cuckoo, cuckoo!--O word of fear,
Unpleasing to a married ear!

William Shakespeare

St. Crispin's Day Speech: from Henry V

WESTMORELAND. O that we now had here
But one ten thousand of those men in England
That do no work to-day!

KING. What's he that wishes so?
My cousin Westmoreland? No, my fair cousin;
If we are mark'd to die, we are enow
To do our country loss; and if to live,
The fewer men, the greater share of honour.
God's will! I pray thee, wish not one man more.
By Jove, I am not covetous for gold,
Nor care I who doth feed upon my cost;
It yearns me not if men my

garments wear;
Such outward things dwell not in
my desires.
But if it be a sin to covet honour,
I am the most offending soul alive.
No, faith, my coz, wish not a man
from England.
God's peace! I would not lose so
great an honour
As one man more methinks would
share from me
For the best hope I have. O, do not
wish one more!
Rather proclaim it, Westmoreland,
through my host,
That he which hath no stomach to
this fight,
Let him depart; his passport shall
be made,
And crowns for convoy put into his
purse;
We would not die in that man's
company
That fears his fellowship to die with
us.

This day is call'd the feast of
Crispian.
He that outlives this day, and
comes safe home,
Will stand a tip-toe when this day is
nam'd,
And rouse him at the name of
Crispian.
He that shall live this day, and see
old age,
Will yearly on the vigil feast his
neighbours,
And say "To-morrow is Saint
Crispian."
Then will he strip his sleeve and
show his scars,
And say "These wounds I had on
Crispian's day."
Old men forget; yet all shall be
forgot,
But he'll remember, with
advantages,
What feats he did that day. Then
shall our names,
Familiar in his mouth as household

words-
Harry the King, Bedford and
Exeter,
Warwick and Talbot, Salisbury and
Gloucester-
Be in their flowing cups freshly
rememb'red.
This story shall the good man
teach his son;
And Crispin Crispian shall ne'er go
by,
From this day to the ending of the
world,
But we in it shall be remembered-
We few, we happy few, we band of
brothers;
For he to-day that sheds his blood
with me
Shall be my brother; be he ne'er so
vile,
This day shall gentle his condition;
And gentlemen in England now-a-
bed
Shall think themselves accurs'd
they were not here,

And hold their manhoods cheap
whiles any speaks
That fought with us upon Saint
Crispin's day.

William Shakespeare

Sweet-and-Twenty

O MISTRESS mine, where are you
roaming?
O, stay and hear! your true love 's
coming,
That can sing both high and low:
Trip no further, pretty sweeting;
Journeys end in lovers meeting,
Every wise man's son doth know.

What is love? 'tis not hereafter;
Present mirth hath present
laughter;
What 's to come is still unsure:
In delay there lies no plenty;
Then come kiss me, sweet-and-
twenty!
Youth 's a stuff will not endure.

William Shakespeare

Take, O take those Lips away

TAKE, O take those lips away,
That so sweetly were forsworn;
And those eyes, the break of day,
Lights that do mislead the morn!
But my kisses bring again,
Bring again;
Seals of love, but seal'd in vain,
Seal'd in vain!

William Shakespeare

Blossom

ON a day--alack the day!--
Love, whose month is ever May,
Spied a blossom passing fair
Playing in the wanton air:
Through the velvet leaves the wind
All unseen 'gan passage find;
That the lover, sick to death,
Wish'd himself the heaven's breath.
Air, quoth he, thy cheeks may
blow;
Air, would I might triumph so!
But, alack, my hand is sworn
Ne'er to pluck thee from thy thorn:
Vow, alack, for youth unmeet;
Youth so apt to pluck a sweet!
Do not call it sin in me
That I am forsworn for thee;
Thou for whom e'en Jove would
swear
Juno but an Ethiop were;
And deny himself for Jove,
Turning mortal for thy love.

William Shakespeare

The Passionate Pilgrim

I.

When my love swears that she is
made of truth,
I do believe her, though I know she
lies,
That she might think me some
untutor'd youth,
Unskilful in the world's false
forgeries,
Thus vainly thinking that she thinks
me young,
Although I know my years be past
the best,
I smiling credit her false-speaking
tongue,
Outfacing faults in love with love's
ill rest.
But wherefore says my love that
she is young?
And wherefore say not I that I am
old?
O, love's best habit is a soothing

tongue,
And age, in love, loves not to have
years told.
Therefore, I'll lie with love, and love
with me,
Since that our faults in love thus
smother'd be.

II.
Two loves I have, of comfort and
despair,
That like two spirits do suggest me
still;
My better angel is a man right fair,
My worser spirit a woman colour'd
ill.
To win me soon to hell, my female
evil
Tempteth my better angel from my
side,
And would corrupt my saint to be a
devil,
Wooing his purity with her fair
pride.
And whether that my angel be

turn'd fiend,
Suspect I may, yet not directly tell:
For being both to me, both to each
friend,
I guess one angel in another's hell:
The truth I shall not know, but live
in doubt,
Till my bad angel fire my good one
out.

III.
Did not the heavenly rhetoric of
thine eye,
'Gainst whom the world could not
hold argument.
Persuade my heart to this false
perjury?
Vows for thee broke deserve not
punishment.
A woman I forswore; but I will
prove,
Thou being a goddess, I forswore
not thee:
My vow was earthly, thou a
heavenly love:

Thy grace being gain'd cures all
disgrace in me.
My vow was breath, and breath a
vapour is;
Then, thou fair sun, that on this
earth doth shine,
Exhale this vapour vow; in thee it
is:
If broken, then it is no fault of mine.
If by me broke, what fool is not so
wise
To break an oath, to win a
paradise?

IV.
Sweet Cytherea, sitting by a brook
With young Adonis, lovely, fresh,
and green,
Did court the lad with many a lovely
look,
Such looks as none could look but
beauty's queen,
She told him stories to delight his
ear;
She show'd him favours to allure

his eye;
To win his heart, she touch'd him
here and there, --
Touches so soft still conquer
chastity.
But whether unripe years did want
conceit,
Or he refused to take her figured
proffer,
The tender nibbler would not touch
the bait,
But smile and jest at every gentle
offer:
Then fell she on her back, fair
queen, and toward:
He rose and ran away; ah, fool too
froward!

V.

If love make me forsworn, how
shall I swear to love?
O never faith could hold, if not to
beauty vow'd:
Though to myself forsworn, to thee
I'll constant prove;

Those thoughts, to me like oaks, to
thee like osiers bow'd.
Study his bias leaves, and make
his book thine eyes,
Where all those pleasures live that
art can comprehend.
If knowledge be the mark, to know
thee shall suffice;
Well learned is that tongue that
well can thee commend;
All ignorant that soul that sees thee
without wonder;
Which is to me some praise, that I
thy parts admire:
Thy eye Jove's lightning seems,
thy voice his dreadful thunder,
Which, not to anger bent, is music
and sweet fire.
Celestial as thou art, O do not love
that wrong,
To sing heaven's praise with such
an earthly tongue.

VI.
Scarce had the sun dried up the

dewy morn,
And scarce the herd gone to the
hedge for shade,
When Cytherea, all in love forlorn,
A longing tarriance for Adonis
made
Under an osier growing by a brook,
A brook where Adon used to cool
his spleen:
Hot was the day; she hotter that did
look
For his approach, that often there
had been.
Anon he comes, and throws his
mantle by,
And stood stark naked on the
brook's green brim:
The sun look'd on the world with
glorious eye,
Yet not so wistly as this queen on
him.
He, spying her, bounced in,
whereas he stood:
'O Jove,' quoth she, 'why was not I
a flood!'

VII.

Fair is my love, but not so fair as
fickle;
Mild as a dove, but neither true nor
trusty;
Brighter than glass, and yet, as
glass is brittle;
Softer than wax, and yet, as iron,
rusty:
A lily pale, with damask dye to
grace her,
None fairer, nor none falser to
deface her.

Her lips to mine how often hath she
joined,
Between each kiss her oaths of
true love swearing!
How many tales to please me bath
she coined,
Dreading my love, the loss thereof
still fearing!
Yet in the midst of all her pure
protestings,

Her faith, her oaths, her tears, and
all were jestings.

She burn'd with love, as straw with
fire flameth;
She burn'd out love, as soon as
straw outburneth;
She framed the love, and yet she
foil'd the framing;
She bade love last, and yet she fell
a-turning.
Was this a lover, or a lecher
whether?
Bad in the best, though excellent in
neither.

VIII.
If music and sweet poetry agree,
As they must needs, the sister and
the brother,
Then must the love be great 'twixt
thee and me,
Because thou lovest the one, and I
the other.
Dowland to thee is dear, whose

heavenly touch
Upon the lute doth ravish human
sense;
Spenser to me, whose deep
conceit is such
As, passing all conceit, needs no
defence.
Thou lovest to bear the sweet
melodious sound
That Phoebus' lute, the queen of
music, makes;
And I in deep delight am chiefly
drown'd
Whenas himself to singing he
betakes.
One god is god of both, as poets
feign;
One knight loves both, and both in
thee remain.

IX.
Fair was the morn when the fair
queen of love,
Paler for sorrow than her milk-white
dove,

For Adon's sake, a youngster
proud and wild;
Her stand she takes upon a steep-
up hill:
Anon Adonis comes with horn and
hounds;
She, silly queen, with more than
love's good will,
Forbade the boy he should not
pass those grounds:
'Once,' quoth she, 'did I see a fair
sweet youth
Here in these brakes deep-
wounded with a boar,
Deep in the thigh, a spectacle of
ruth!
See, in my thigh,' quoth she, 'here
was the sore.
She showed hers: he saw more
wounds than one,
And blushing fled, and left her all
alone.

X.

Sweet rose, fair flower, untimely

pluck'd, soon vaded,
Pluck'd in the bud, and vaded in
the spring!
Bright orient pearl, alack, too timely
shaded!
Fair creature, kill'd too soon by
death's sharp sting!
Like a green plum that hangs upon
a tree,
And falls, through wind, before the
fall should he.

I weep for thee, and yet no cause I
have;
For why thou left'st me nothing in
thy will:
And yet thou left'st me more than I
did crave;
For why I craved nothing of thee
still:
O yes, dear friend, I pardon crave
of thee,
Thy discontent thou didst bequeath
to me.

XI.

Venus, with young Adonis sitting by
her
Under a myrtle shade, began to
woo him:
She told the youngling how god
Mars did try her,
And as he fell to her, so fell she to
him.
'Even thus,' quoth she, 'the warlike
god embraced me,'
And then she clipp'd Adonis in her
arms;
'Even thus,' quoth she, 'the warlike
god unlaced me,'
As if the boy should use like loving
charms;
'Even thus,' quoth she, 'he seized
on my lips
And with her lips on his did act the
seizure
And as she fetched breath, away
he skips,
And would not take her meaning
nor her pleasure.

Ah, that I had my lady at this bay,
To kiss and clip me till I run away!

XII.

Crabbed age and youth cannot live
together
Youth is full of pleasance, age is
full of care;
Youth like summer morn, age like
winter weather;
Youth like summer brave, age like
winter bare;
Youth is full of sport, age's breath
is short;
Youth is nimble, age is lame;
Youth is hot and bold, age is weak
and cold;
Youth is wild, and age is tame.
Age, I do abhor thee; youth, I do
adore thee;
O, my love, my love is young!
Age, I do defy thee: O, sweet
shepherd, hie thee,
For methinks thou stay'st too long.

XIII.

Beauty is but a vain and doubtful
good;
A shining gloss that vadeth
suddenly;
A flower that dies when first it gins
to bud;
A brittle glass that's broken
presently:
A doubtful good, a gloss, a glass, a
flower,
Lost, vaded, broken, dead within
an hour.

And as goods lost are seld or never
found,
As vaded gloss no rubbing will
refresh,
As flowers dead lie wither'd on the
ground,
As broken glass no cement can
redress,
So beauty blemish'd once's for
ever lost,
In spite of physic, painting, pain

and cost.

XIV.

Good night, good rest. Ah, neither
be my share:
She bade good night that kept my
rest away;
And daff'd me to a cabin hang'd
with care,
To descant on the doubts of my
decay.
'Farewell,' quoth she, 'and come
again tomorrow:
Fare well I could not, for I supp'd
with sorrow.

Yet at my parting sweetly did she
smile,
In scorn or friendship, nill I
construe whether:
'T may be, she joy'd to jest at my
exile,
'T may be, again to make me
wander thither:
'Wander,' a word for shadows like

myself,
As take the pain, but cannot pluck
the pelf.

XV.

Lord, how mine eyes throw gazes
to the east!
My heart doth charge the watch;
the morning rise
Doth cite each moving sense from
idle rest.
Not daring trust the office of mine
eyes,
While Philomela sits and sings, I sit
and mark,
And wish her lays were tuned like
the lark;

For she doth welcome daylight with
her ditty,
And drives away dark dismal-
dreaming night:
The night so pack'd, I post unto my
pretty;
Heart hath his hope, and eyes their
wished sight;

Sorrow changed to solace, solace mix'd with sorrow;
For why, she sigh'd and bade me come tomorrow.
Were I with her, the night would post too soon;
But now are minutes added to the hours;
To spite me now, each minute seems a moon;
Yet not for me, shine sun to succour flowers!
Pack night, peep day; good day, of night now borrow:
Short, night, to-night, and length thyself tomorrow.

William Shakespeare

The Phoenix and the Turtle

Let the bird of loudest lay,
On the sole Arabian tree,
Herald sad and trumpet be,
To whose sound chaste wings
obey.

But thou, shrieking harbinger,
Foul pre-currer of the fiend,
Augur of the fever's end,
To this troop come thou not near.

From this session interdict
Every fowl of tyrant wing,
Save the eagle, feather'd king:
Keep the obsequy so strict.

Let the priest in surplice white,
That defunctive music can,
Be the death-defying swan,
Lest the requiem lack his right.

And thou, treble-dated crow,
That thy sable gender mak'st

With the breath thou giv'st and
tak'st,
'Mongst our mourners shalt thou
go.

Here the anthem doth commence:
Love and constancy is dead;
Phoenix and the turtle fled
In a mutual flame from hence.

So they lov'd, as love in twain
Had the essence but in one;
Two distincts, division none:
Number there in love was slain.

Hearts remote, yet not asunder;
Distance, and no space was seen
'Twixt the turtle and his queen;
But in them it were a wonder.

So between them love did shine,
That the turtle saw his right
Flaming in the phoenix' sight:
Either was the other's mine.

Property was thus appall'd,
That the self was not the same;
Single nature's double name
Neither two nor one was call'd.

Reason, in itself confounded,
Saw division grow together;
To themselves yet either-neither,
Simple were so well compounded.

That it cried how true a twain
Seemeth this concordant one!
Love hath reason, reason none
If what parts can so remain.

Whereupon it made this threne
To the phoenix and the dove,
Co-supreme and stars of love;
As chorus to their tragic scene.

THRENOS.

Beauty, truth, and rarity.
Grace in all simplicity,
Here enclos'd in cinders lie.

Death is now the phoenix' nest;
And the turtle's loyal breast
To eternity doth rest,

Leaving no posterity:--
'Twas not their infirmity,
It was married chastity.

Truth may seem, but cannot be:
Beauty brag, but 'tis not she;
Truth and beauty buried be.

To this urn let those repair
That are either true or fair;
For these dead birds sigh a prayer.

William Shakespeare

The Quality of Mercy

The quality of mercy is not strain'd.
It droppeth as the gentle rain from
heaven
Upon the place beneath. It is twice
blest:
It blesseth him that gives, and him
that takes.
'Tis mightiest in the mightiest; it
becomes
The throned monarch better than
his crown.
His scepter shows the force of
temporal power,
The attribute to awe and majesty,
Wherein doth sit the dread and fear
of kings;
But mercy is above this sceptered
sway;

It is enthroned in the heart of kings;
It is an attribute to God himself;
And earthly power doth then show
likest God's
When mercy seasons justice.

William Shakespeare

To be, or not to be: that is the question

To be, or not to be: that is the
question:
Whether 'tis nobler in the mind to
suffer
The slings and arrows of
outrageous fortune,
Or to take arms against a sea of
troubles,
And by opposing end them?
To die: to sleep;
No more; and, by a sleep to say we
end
The heart-ache and the thousand
natural shocks
That flash is heir to, tis a
consummation
Devoutly to be wished.
To die, to sleep;
To sleep erchance to dream:ay,
there's the rub;
For in that sleep of death what
dreams may come

When we have shuffled off this
mortal coil,
Must give us pause.
There's the respect
That makes calamity of so long life;
For who would bear the whips and
scorns of time,
The pangs of disprized love, the
law's delay,
The insolence of office, and the
spurns
That patient merit of the unworthy
takes,
When he himself might his quietus
make
With a bare bodkin?
Who would fardels bear,
To grunt and sweat under a weary
life,
But that the dread of something
after death,
The undiscovered country from
whose bourn
No traveller returns, puzzles the
will,

And make us rather bear those ills
we have
Than fly to others that we know not
of?
Thus conscience does make
cowards of us all;
And Is sicklied o'er
With the pale cast of thought
And enterprises of great pith and
moment
With this regard their currents turn
away,
And lose the name of action.

William Shakespeare

To Me, Fair Friend, You Never Can Be Old

To me, fair Friend, you never can
be old,
For as you were when first your
eye I eyed
Such seems your beauty still,
Three winters' cold
Have from the forests shook three
summers' pride;

Three beauteous springs to yellow
autmun turn'd
In process of the seasons have I
seen,
Three April perfumes in three hot
Junes burn'd,
Since first I saw you fresh, which
yet are green.

Ah! yes doth beauty, like a dial-
hand,
Steal from his figure, and no pace
perceived;

So your sweet hue, which methinks
still doth stand,
Hath motion, and mine eye may be
deceived,

For fear of which, hear this, thou
age unbred,-
Ere you were born, was beauty's
summer dead.

William Shakespeare

Twelve O'Clock - Fairy time

Through the house give glimmering
light
By the dead and drowsy fire;
Every elf and fairy sprite
hop as light as bird from brier.

Now, until the break of day
Through this house each fairy
stray.

William Shakespeare

Under the Greenwood Tree

Under the greenwood tree
Who loves to lie with me,
And turn his merry note
Unto the sweet bird's throat,
Come hither, come hither, come
hither:
Here shall he see
No enemy
But winter and rough weather.

Who doth ambition shun,
And loves to live i' the sun,
Seeking the food he eats,
And pleas'd with what he gets,
Come hither, come hither, come
hither:
Here shall he see
No enemy
But winter and rough weather.

William Shakespeare

When that I was and a little tiny boy

When that I was and a little tiny
boy,
With hey, ho, the wind and the rain,
A foolish thing was but a toy,
For the rain it raineth every day.

But when I came to man's estate,
With hey, ho, . . .
'Gainst knaves and thieves men
shut their gate
For the rain, . . .

But when I came, alas! to wive,
With hey, ho, . . .
By swaggering could I never thrive,
For the rain, . . .

But when I came unto my beds,
With hey, ho, . . .
With toss-pots still had drunken
heads,
For the rain, . . .

211

A great while ago the world begun,
With hey, ho, . . .
But that's all one, our play is done.
And we'll strive to please you every
day.

William Shakespeare

Winter

When icicles hang by the wall
And Dick the shepherd blows his
nail
And Tom bears logs into the hall,
And milk comes frozen home in
pail,
When Blood is nipped and ways be
foul,
Then nightly sings the staring owl,
Tu-who;
Tu-whit, tu-who: a merry note,
While greasy Joan doth keel the
pot.

When all aloud the wind doth blow,
And coughing drowns the parson's
saw,
And birds sit brooding in the snow,
And Marian's nose looks red and
raw
When roasted crabs hiss in the
bowl,
Then nightly sings the staring owl,

Tu-who;
Tu-whit, tu-who: a merry note,
While greasy Joan doth keel the
pot.

William Shakespeare

Sonnets 110

Alas, 'tis true I have gone here and
there
And made myself a motley to the
view,
Gor'd mine own thoughts, sold
cheap what is most dear,
Made old offences of affections
new.
Most true it is that I have look'd on
truth
Askance and strangely: but, by all
above,
These blenches gave my heart
another youth,
And worse essays prov'd thee my
best of love.
Now all is done, have what shall
have no end!
Mine appetite, I never more will
grind
On newer proof, to try an older
friend,
A god in love, to whom I am

confin'd.
Then give me welcome, next my
heaven the best,
Even to thy pure and most most
loving breast.

William Shakespeare

Sonnets 146

Poor soul, the centre of my sinful earth,

[......] these rebel powers that thee array,

Why dost thou pine within and suffer dearth,

Painting thy outward walls so costly gay?

Why so large cost, having so short a lease,

Dost thou upon thy fading mansion spend?

Shall worms, inheritors of this excess,

Eat up thy charge? Is this thy body's end?

Then soul, live thou upon thy servant's loss

And let that pine to aggravate thy store;

Buy terms divine in selling hours of dross;

Within be fed, without be rich no

more.
So shalt thou feed on Death, that
feeds on men,
And, Death once dead, there's no
more dying then.

Sonnets 16

Let me not to the marriage of true
minds
Admit impediments. Love is not
love
Which alters when it alteration
finds,
Or bends with the remover to
remove.
O no! it is an ever-fixed mark
That looks on tempests and is
never shaken;
It is the star to every wand'ring
bark,
Whose worth's unknown, although
his height be taken.
Love's not Time's fool, though rosy
lips and cheeks
Within his bending sickle's
compass come;
Love alters not with his brief hours
and weeks,
But bears it out even to the edge of
doom.

If this be error and upon me prov'd,
I never writ, nor no man ever lov'd.

William Shakespeare

Sonnet 19

Devouring Time, blunt thou the
lion's paws,
And make the earth devour her
own sweet brood;
Pluck the keen teeth from the fierce
tiger's jaws,
And burn the long-liv'd Phoenix in
her blood;
Make glad and sorry seasons as
thou fleets,
And do whate'er thou wilt, swift-
footed Time,
To the wide world and all her
fading sweets;
But I forbid thee one more heinous
crime:
O, carve not with the hours my
love's fair brow,
Nor draw no lines there with thine
antique pen!
Him in thy course untainted do
allow
For beauty's pattern to succeeding

men.
Yet do thy worst, old Time! Despite thy wrong
My love shall in my verse ever live young.

William Shakespeare

Shakespeare Quotations on Love

My bounty is as boundless as the
sea,
My love as deep; the more I give to
thee,
The more I have, for both are
infinite.
(*Romeo and Juliet*, 2.2.139-41)

Hear my soul speak:
The very instant that I saw you, did
My heart fly to your service.
(*The Tempest*, 3.1.60-3)

Who ever loved that loved not at
first sight?
(*As You Like It*, 3.5.84)

This bud of love, by summer's
ripening breath,
May prove a beauteous flower
when next we meet.
(*Romeo and Juliet*, 2.2.121-2)

Love looks not with the eyes, but with the mind,
And therefore is winged Cupid painted blind.
(*A Midsummer Night's Dream*, 1.1.231-2)

If thou remember'st not the slightest folly
That ever love did make thee run into,
Thou hast not loved.
(*As You Like It*, 2.4.33-5)

Let me not to the marriage of true minds
Admit impediments. Love is not love
Which alters when it alteration finds,
Or bends with the remover to remove:
O no! it is an ever-fixed mark
That looks on tempests and is

never shaken;
It is the star to every wandering
bark,
Whose worth's unknown, although
his height be taken.
Love's not Time's fool, though rosy
lips and cheeks
Within his bending sickle's
compass come:
Love alters not with his brief hours
and weeks,
But bears it out even to the edge of
doom.
If this be error and upon me
proved,
I never writ, nor no man ever loved.
(Sonnet 116)

Eternity was in our lips and eyes,
Bliss in our brows' bent; none our
parts so poor
But was a race of heaven.
(*Antony and Cleopatra*, 1.3.36-8)

Doubt thou the stars are fire;

Doubt that the sun doth move;
Doubt truth to be a liar;
But never doubt I love.
(*Hamlet*, 1.2.123-6)

Have I caught thee, my heavenly
jewel? Why, now let
me die, for I have lived long
enough.
(*The Merry Wives of Windsor*,
3.3.35-6)

Such is my love, to thee I so
belong,
That for thy right myself will bear all
wrong.
(Sonnet 88)

But love, first learned in a lady's
eyes,
Lives not alone immured in the
brain;
But, with the motion of all
elements,
Courses as swift as thought in

every power,
And gives to every power a double
power,
Above their functions and their
offices.
(*Love's Labours Lost*, 4.3.327-55)

See how she leans her cheek upon
her hand.
O that I were a glove upon that
hand,
That I might touch that cheek.
(*Romeo and Juliet*, 2.2.23-5)

One half of me is yours, the other
half yours
Mine own, I would say; but if mine,
then yours,
And so all yours.
(*The Merchant of Venice*, 3.2.17-9)

The sight of lovers feedeth those in
love.
(*As You Like It*, 3.4.54)

I love thee so, that, maugre all thy
pride,
Nor wit nor reason can my passion
hide.
Do not extort thy reasons from this
clause,
For that I woo, thou therefore hast
no cause
But rather reason thus with reason
fetter,
Love sought is good, but given
unsought better.
(*Twelfth Night*, 3.1.151-6)

The prize of all too precious you.
(Sonnet 86)

Shall I compare thee to a summer's
day?
Thou art more lovely and more
temperate:
Rough winds do shake the darling
buds of May,
And summer's lease hath all too
short a date:

Sometime too hot the eye of
heaven shines,
And often is his gold complexion
dimm'd;
And every fair from fair sometime
declines,
By chance or nature's changing
course untrimm'd;
But thy eternal summer shall not
fade
Nor lose possession of that fair
thou owest;
Nor shall Death brag thou
wander'st in his shade,
When in eternal lines to time thou
growest:
So long as men can breathe or
eyes can see,
So long lives this and this gives life
to thee.
(Sonnet 18)

What made me love thee? let that
persuade thee
there's something extraordinary in

thee. I cannot: but I love thee; none but thee; and thou deservest it.
(*The Merry Wives of Windsor*, 3.3.59...)

For thy sweet love remember'd such wealth brings
That then I scorn to change my state with kings.
(Sonnet 29)

All days are nights to see till I see thee,
And nights bright days when dreams do show thee me.
(Sonnet 43)

But, mistress, know yourself: down on your knees,
And thank heaven, fasting, for a good man's love.
(*As You Like It*, 3.5.60-1)

Love is a smoke made with the fumes of sighs;

Being purged, a fire sparkling in
lovers' eyes;
Being vexed, a sea nourished with
lovers' tears;
What is it else? A madness most
discreet,
A choking gall, and a preserving
sweet.
(*Romeo and Juliet*, 1.1.191-5)

Love is a spirit all compact of fire.
(*Venus and Adonis, 151*)

She never told her love,
But let concealment, like a worm
i'th' bud,
Feed on her damask cheek. She
pined in thought,
And with a green and yellow
melancholy
She sat like Patience on a
monument,
Smiling at grief. Was not this love
indeed?
(*Twelfth Night*, 2.4.115-120)

WILLIAM SHAKESPEARE'S

POEMS AND QUOTES

Printed in Great Britain
by Amazon